HEIDEGGER

FOR BEGINNERS

Eric Lemay
and
Jennifer A. Pitts

Illustrated by
Paul Gordon

Orient BlackSwan

HEIDEGGER FOR BEGINNERS

ORIENT BLACKSWAN PRIVATE LIMITED

Registered Office
3-6-752 Himayatnagar, Hyderabad 500 029 (A.P.), INDIA
e-mail: centraloffice@orientblackswan.com

Other Offices
Bangalore, Bhopal, Bhubaneshwar, Chennai, Ernakulam, Guwahati, Hyderabad, Jaipur, Kolkata, Lucknow, Mumbai, New Delhi, Patna

Cover Illustration: Paul Gordon
Cover and book design: Terrie Dunkelberger
This cover: Bindia Thapar

Published by arrangement with
Writers and Readers Limited
PO Box 29522
London NI 8 FB

First published in India by
Orient Longman Private Limited 2005
First Orient Blackswan impression 2010

ISBN 13: 978 81 250 2899 4
ISBN 10: 81 250 2899 4

Printed in India at
Glorious Printers
Delhi

Published by
Orient Blackswan Private Limited
1/24 Asaf Ali Road, New Delhi 110 002
e-mail: delhi@orientblackswan.com

To Dr. James Edwards and Dr. Albert Mosley:

"Yet releasement toward things and openness to the mystery never happen of themselves. They do not befall us accidentally. Both flourish only through persistent, courageous thinking."

Heidegger Memorial Address

Introduction and Background 1

The Ancient Greeks 7

Descartes 13

From Rousseau to Kant 17

Nietzsche 21

Kierkegaard and Husserl 25

...enter Heidegger 28

Being 33

"*Dasein*" 43

The One 49

Existentialism 60

The Thinking Thing: Human-Centered Philosophy 70

Technology and Authenticity 81

Language — "the house of Being" 86

"To be." 94

Heidegger's Influence 98

Heidegger & Nazism 102

Further Reading...105

A sampling of Heidegger's works available in English................106

Man... is not merely a living creature possessing among other faculties that of language. Language is rather the house of Being and man exists dwelling therein as he guards the truth of Being to which he belongs.

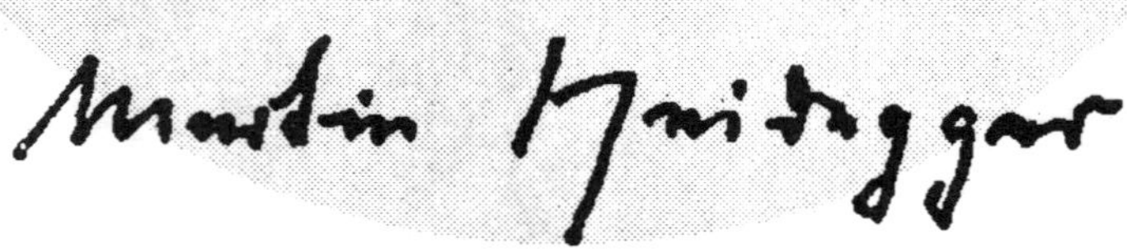

At a secluded cottage in Germany's Black Forest region, a thinker presents us with the challenge of our modern age. . .
"Technology... will never allow itself to be overcome by man. That would mean, after all, that man was the master of Being."
According to Heidegger, philosophy's focus on humanity has helped cause the crisis of the modern world...

Rather than recognizing our place in the world, our status as one being among all other beings, we have turned the world into something that exists for and because of us. Through our arrogance, we have turned the earth into an expendable resource...
Disposable
EARTH
NET WT. 2 MIL. TONS

We treat the world and everything in it as something to be *consumed*...
"One type of being, the human being, believes that all of Being exists for it."

The world and everything in it exists to be *used*—by *us!* Why? Because we are human; because we give the world its "frame of reference"; because we *think*.

Many of the world's atrocities can be traced back to the supposedly harmless philosophical belief that we human beings are *special*, that we somehow provide reference to the world, that we are what Descartes called "thinking things."
AM I S'POSED TO TAKE YOUR WORD FOR THAT?
In order to understand the connection between human-centered philosophy, our technological world view, and Being, one must first understand Descartes' famous statement, "I think, therefore I am"... but, of course, one can't fully comprehend Descartes without foreknowledge of the ancient Greeks, which, in turn...
HOLD IT! THIS IS SUPPOSED TO BE A CLEAR AND ACCESSIBLE INTRODUCTION TO YOUR PHILOSOPHY! NOW, GET WITH THE PROGRAM!
To get a clear picture of my ideas, it helps to understand the traditional Western philosophy from which they evolved...
O.K., BUT JUST GIVE ME THE GREATEST HITS!
HEIDEGGER
Greatest Hits!

For a clear understanding of Heidegger's philosophy, it is necessary to go back a few thousand years and familiarize ourselves with some of the ancient Greeks who started things off by asking a few nagging questions. . .

THE UNEXAMINED LIFE IS NOT WORTH LIVING.
CAN WE COME TO KNOW THAT WHICH DOES NOT EXIST?
HOW DO WE COMPREHEND A WORLD THAT CONSTANTLY CHANGES?
COULD MATHEMATICS LIE AT THE CORE OF THE UNIVERSE?
SOCRATES
PARMENIDES
PYTHAGORAS
HERACLITUS
Plato (428-354)
While people have been trying to answer such questions long before and long after these thinkers, it was Plato, the great philosopher, who first set up a systematic way of answering—and asking—them.
MY WORK IS WRITTEN IN DIALOGUES, STARRING SOCRATES (470-399 B.C.), MY TEACHER. CONSEQUENTLY, IT IS DIFFICULT FOR HISTORIANS TO SEPARATE MY IDEAS FROM HIS.

Plato came up with a **Theory of Ideas** to account for all of the various things in the universe. Everything that exists—books, horses, trees, etc.—derives its shape and meaning from its **Form**. Forms are the perfect, eternal *ideas* of things that everyday objects copy.

For example, outside of time and space there exists the Form of a book. This Form has every quality that goes along with our idea of a book. It is the Perfect Book, the ultimate in bookness.

All other books are merely inferior copies modeled from this Form.

According to Plato, each existing thing has a Form. Forms not only exist for books and trees but also for abstract ideas like Justice, Beauty, Truth and the Good. Thus, every object and every idea can be judged by comparison to its original Form. The big problem: How do we know about these Forms if they exist outside of time and space? Plato answered this by stating that every human goes through a process called "**anamnesis**," multiple cycles of life and death, of "bodied and disembodied states."
PLATO'S TUNNEL OF ANAMNESIS
WHAT A RIDE! LET'S DO IT AGAIN!

During each disembodied state, we know the Forms but, to our chagrin, we forget about them at birth. However, through the use of reason, we are able to slowly recall all our disembodied knowledge.
ORIGINAL!
FORMS
PERFECT MODELS!!!
TICKETS
I THINK I'VE SEEN THESE BEFORE...
...NOT IN THIS LIFETIME.

Students do not learn knowledge, they remember it...
BIOLOGY DISSECTION TODAY
HAVEN'T WE MET SOMEWHERE BEFORE?
...and scientists do not make discoveries, they recall their knowledge.
I KNEW THAT WAS GOING TO HAPPEN.
A REAL KNOW-IT-ALL!
Consequently, philosophers, as persons of reason, are closest to eternal knowledge and, Plato would add, are best fit to rule. (Plato envisioned a world run by philosophers instead of politicians!)

It was Plato's thinking that got the big ball of philosophy rolling...

...a ball that would be responsible for crumbling empires, inciting revolutions and catalyzing the greatest achievements of humankind. Not bad for a guy in a sheet!

Over the next two-thousand years, a long and distinguished list of philosophers would refine, refute and transform Plato's original views by asking and answering those essential human questions over and over again.

Our next important figure, **René Descartes** (1596-1650), developed a system so far-reaching that he has been dubbed "the father of modern philosophy." Descartes didn't like uncertainty. He wanted his philosophical system to be as precise and free from doubt as mathematics or science. To do so, he needed an "absolute axiom" [something that was, beyond any doubt, **true**] upon which to base his system of knowledge. So he began by questioning *everything*—a process he called **Radical Doubt**.

In the first step of this process of Radical Doubt, Descartes examined knowledge derived from the senses. The senses, it turns out, are rather dubious things. While they *seem* to produce almost all of our knowledge, they cannot be trusted. For example...

IS THIS WATER ON THE HIGHWAY?

TWO FACES OR A VASE?

DOES A STRAW REALLY BEND IN WATER?

So, for Descartes, all sensory knowledge had to go. This, however, seemed a bit extreme, even to Descartes. After all, it would be absurd to deny the reality of everything around us.

Descartes approached the problem again from another angle—dreams. Things we see every day *appear* real in our dreams, and, while we are dreaming, we cannot tell that these things are merely images in our imagination.

From the dream perspective, all sensory knowledge was questionable. Descartes had to look elsewhere to find absolute certainty.
Having to resort to something not based on the senses, Descartes turned to his old standby, mathematics. Surely, whether he was awake or in a dream, 2+2=4. To obtain absolute knowledge, to be *absolutely* certain, Descartes had to consider every possibility...
I COULD DO THIS IN MY SLEEP!
How can we prove, Descartes wondered, that the universe is not controlled by an evil demon who deceives us, making even the most obvious mathematical truths unreliable?
Since such a possibility existed, Descartes ruled out mathematics as an absolute form of knowledge. Since both sensory and non-sensory knowledge were uncertain, Descartes concluded that there was only one thing beyond doubt. Regardless of whether he was awake or dreaming, regardless of whether an evil demon was tricking him or not, regardless of whether or not all his thoughts were false, **he did think.** Whether he was dreaming or whether he was really an isolated brain in a vat being fed information, he did have thoughts. It was this idea that spawned the famous saying...
...HOW COULD OSWALD HAVE ACTED ALONE?...

I Think, Therefore I Am.

Descartes had found his *absolute axiom*, his foundation for absolute knowledge—the **Thinking Thing**. From there he went on to construct a system of knowledge that accounted for the world, God, others and mathematics.

- The Thinking Thing exists
- God exists, because we can conceive of him
- A benevolent God precludes the possibility of an evil demon so mathematics must exist
- Using the principles of mathematics, we can derive the outside world

...and so on.

However, this philosophical system, like every other, would be criticized by philosophers to come.

Jean-Jacques Rousseau (1712-1778)

Roughly one-hundred years after Descartes postulated this rather abstract Thinking Thing, another philosopher, **Jean-Jacques Rousseau,** took this Thing and gave it a more romantic flair. Walking through the woods of St. Germain, Rousseau came to realize his true inner nature: a nature full of goodness, harmonious with the rest of the natural world. He felt that humans were not cold, analytic things, but rather creatures isolated from their true natures by the constraints of modern society. Rousseau called this core of human nature the **Self**.

This Self, however, was so deep, so rich, so full of goodness, so darn wonderful that Rousseau felt it had to be something more than just his own *self*. Having decided that he must have tapped into a universal soul, Rousseau felt he could come to know the nature of all humanity

simply by examining the intricacies of his own mind. Rousseau and his followers caused such a backlash that a new school of philosophy emerged, asserting that Rousseau was a deluded idealist.

These thinkers, called the **Empiricists** [empirical=based on experience or observation], denied the grandiose assumptions of Descartes and Rousseau and opted for a more common-sense view of the world. The followers of Descartes and Rousseau, called the **Rationalists**, argued that the empirical viewpoint ignored the role of the mind in witnessing, recording and analyzing sensory experience. The brawl between Empiricism and Rationalism continued until the end of the 18th century, when it was resolved by the German philosopher **Immanuel Kant.**

Kant proclaimed that the Self had innate structures that it used to take in all sensory information. He agreed with the Empiricists' claim that sensory experience is where we derive our knowledge but, at the same time, he gave the Rationalists credit for realizing that the human mind filters every experience in its own unique way.

Kant (1724-1804)

Every experience, for Kant, was first and foremost a **human** experience. We cannot deny that when *we* look, for example, at a flower, we look at it in a peculiarly human way. We cannot know what the flower is like apart from our experience of it.

Along with structures like Time and Space, Kant came up with categories such as Unity, Reality, Substance and Possibility, which all help filter experience. Kant presumed that we all have the same filters and, thus, by examining the categories of his own mind, Kant believed, like Rousseau, that he could generate universal human knowledge.

In the realm of ethics, Kant believed that all moral behavior could be generated from a principle that he called the **Categorical Imperative**.

While Kant's Categorical Imperative does not seem too practical from a common-sense view, many of the situations where it would have to be violated would not arise if, according to Kant, everyone followed it. One of the main arguments brought against Kant was that his philosophy was simply too neat, that it denied the way things really are. In attempting to develop a flawless, hermetic system to explain the world, Kant ignored everyday facts. Like: people don't always tell the truth, the whole truth, and nothing but the truth...

The philosopher who took this line of critique to the extreme was the infamous **Friedrich Nietzsche** (1844-1900). Nietzsche argued that Kant's tidy philosophy exemplified the most far-reaching false assumption in the history of philosophy: namely, that some sort of universal "truth" existed to be discovered.

While our initial intuitions would seem to disagree with Nietzsche, his claims make more sense when we look at certain historical events.

The Vietnam War

Manifest Destiny

Nietzsche thought that the most coercive and oppressive dogma of his time that laid claim to absolute truth was Christianity. He thought that Christianity reduced humanity to the lowest common denominator. The Christians preached doctrines such as "all should be humble before the church" and "all of one's energy should be used to help the less fortunate." Nietzsche considered that way of life absurd.
"Has any great feat ever been accomplished by someone who acts like a meager Christian? Could Michaelangelo have painted or Caesar conquered the world if they had lived a life bowing down before others? Great accomplishments take great efforts. The Christians wouid have us be a world of humble toads scurrying along the ground sacrificing all pleasure, strength and happiness for some 'afterlife.' None of this is truth. God is dead!"
All the laws, canons, rights and doctrines of groups claiming truth, according to Nietzsche, were ways of oppressing our higher instincts.
NO DANCING! NO BOOZE! NO SEX! GIVE ME SOME DOUGH!
NO CIVIL DISOBEDIENCE! NO INFORMATION! NO ART! GIVE ME SOME DOUGH!
Only the strong and the noble are capable of creating their own laws and their own ways of life. The rest of us are simply obedient sheep with our noses up the butt of the sheep in front of us, following the herd.
WHERE ARE WE GOING? THIS ISN'T VERY EXCITING. WHO'S LEADING THIS THING ANYWAY?

Nietzsche thought that this sheep mentality—which he called **slave morality**—dragged down the noble and the great into a pit of mediocrity.

Like his denial of absolute truth, Nietzsche rejected conventional moral values. We make our own values or let others make them for us. What we think is truth is really only a kind of prejudice.

Ideas like Kant's universal categories are not truths, but functions of what Nietzsche called **will to power**. In Nietzsche's view, every organism lives to increase its life force—or power—and all "truth" claims depend on this will to power. Truth became simply a matter of "interpretation"—if *you* have the power, we'll interpret it *your* way.

Think of a case in a court of law. Lawyers argue for certain interpretations of the events in order to convince the jury of the "truth" of the matter. If one of the parties has a lot of money or influence—*power*—the "truth" is usually "interpreted" in his favor.

Nietzsche transformed the way philosophers approached questions of knowledge and truth. Truth, even when it wasn't coerced by power, had to be interpreted.

Even our most basic truths depend on interpretation. For example, two parallel lines **do** meet if a geometry system is based on the curve of the earth. Lines parallel at the equator will meet at the poles.

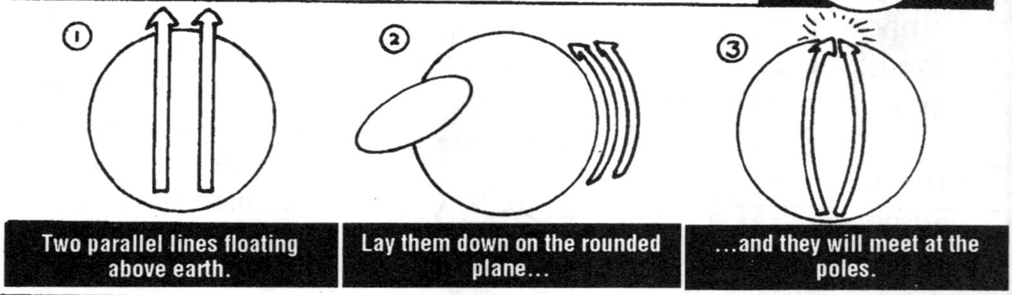

But even before Nietzsche, the Danish philosopher **Soren Kierkegaard** threw into doubt the ideas of truth, knowledge and God. He did this by taking into account *time*, which philosophers before him had considered irrelevant.

Soren Kierkegaard
(1813-1855)

Truth, for Kierkegaard, was subjective. In his view, we cannot know anything universal, anything that transcends time. If there was a timeless truth, we could not comprehend it, because we ourselves are not timeless. Consequently, truth which is relevant for the individual could not be anything greater than the individual. Kierkegaard considered this subjectivity of truth very important.

What about God?

Kierkegaard did not say (as Nietzsche would a few years later) that God is dead.

He said only that we cannot know God exists. Therefore, we must make a leap of faith.

This leap is the way to authentic existence.

Kierkegaard was himself a Christian, but he did not think that going to church and praying had anything to do with being so. Rather, the most noble thing one could do was to bank everything on one's belief, knowing you could never be certain.

While Kierkegaard criticized the philosophical systems that effaced the individual and claimed an objective, timeless knowledge, a half-century later, scientists began making these very claims. The general feeling seemed to be that science was on the verge of solving any problems it had not already solved. Out of this intellectual environment came another rebel, who felt it was his task to debunk these grandiose assumptions, **Edmund Husserl.**

Edmund Husserl (1859-1938)

Husserl believed that scientific knowledge was very useful, **but**, despite this utility, it did not produce the most important kind of knowledge. While we benefit from knowledge about atoms and radio waves, this information does not help us to understand our human concerns. For example, take a scientific approach to love. . .

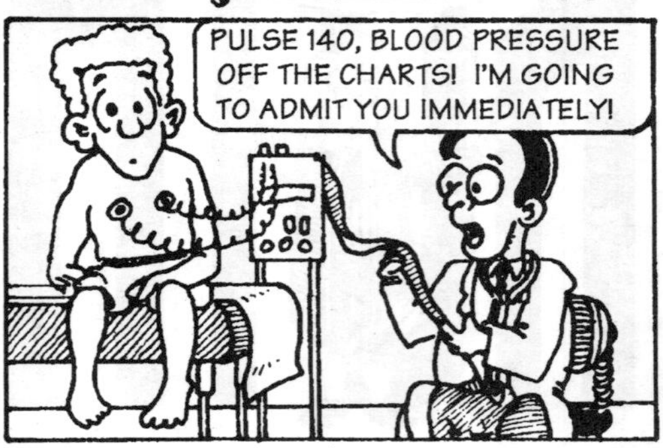

To solve this discrepancy, Husserl developed a philosophical method called **phenomenology**. Using this method, he was able to specifically describe the "experience" or "awareness" of things in a manner which did not reduce them to scientific data. For Husserl, a person's experience was an experience *of something*.

By focusing his attention on the act of this "experiencing of" rather than on the thing being experienced or on the person who was having the experiencing, he produced a new kind of knowledge. This knowledge could account for things unthinkable by science, such as...

Husserl rescued everyday experience from the reductive limitations of science and developed a new, rigorous method of establishing knowledge. This method would inspire many thinkers who felt the scientific approach to the world was impoverished.

One philosopher who felt this way happened to be Husserl's best student, our boy, **Martin Heidegger**. Heidegger not only thought that science was impoverished, he believed the entire philosophical tradition, including his teacher, was misdirected. So much so, in fact, that he claimed his views marked the end of philosophy, a now outdated pursuit, and the beginning of a new task which he called **thinking**. To explicate his views, he engaged, refuted and revised—either directly or indirectly—all the philosophies of the figures we have discussed.

Over the course of his life, Heidegger wrote over fifty volumes of work on almost every conceivable topic, starting in 1914 with his doctoral thesis on the medieval philosopher, Duns Scotus. Heidegger himself, however, started a few years earlier.

On the twenty-sixth of September 1889, Heidegger was born into a strongly Catholic family in the town of Messkirch in the Black Forest region of Balden-Wurtemberg, Germany.
CONGRATULATIONS, MRS. HEIDEGGER, IT'S...A PHILOSOPHER.
Heidegger received his formal philosophical training at the University of Freiburg under Heinrich Rickert, a neo-Kantian, and Edmund Husserl.
DROP, AND GIVE ME 20 PUSHUPS!
STATE
COACH
From 1915 to 1928, Heidegger lectured at both Freiburg and the University of Marburg, establishing a widespread reputation.
MY FRIENDS TOLD ME ALL ABOUT YOU, SO TRY THIS ONE ON FOR SIZE: IF TWO TRAINS HEADING DUE EAST LEAVE THE STATION EXACTLY THIRTY MINUTES APART...

In 1927, Heidegger published his magnum opus, *Being and Time*, which eventually became world renowned. In 1928, as a member of the *Nazi* party, Heidegger succeeded Husserl, a Jew, as chairman at Freiburg. Heidegger actively helped to implement Nazi policy throughout the university. In 1944, by order of Allied authorities, Heidegger was suspended from teaching until 1951.

There is an appendix on Heidegger's Nazism at the end of this book that touches on this topic, but it cannot begin to explain how some people—like the composer Richard Wagner or the poet Ezra Pound—can exhibit such genius in one area while being so politically and morally irresponsible.

After his retirement in 1959, Heidegger left the university environment and returned to Messkirch, where he spent the rest of his life as a recluse. Heidegger died in Messkirch on May 26, 1976.
In my rural existence in the Black Forest, I attempted to live in a way that embodied the values of my philosophy.
The central focus of Heidegger's entire life brings us back to the fundamental mystery of existence. For Heidegger, there was a problem: Ever since philosophers began asking questions about the world, they—all of them—have overlooked its most important fact. Namely, that **the world exists**.

THE WORLD IS A PRODUCT OF OUR MENTAL STRUCTURES.
THE WORLD IS A PHENOMENON OF OUR EXPERIENCE.
THE WORLD IS A GAME OF CHAOS AND POWER.
NO! NO! NO! THE FUNDAMENTAL MYSTERY OF LIFE IS THAT SOMETHING EXISTS, RATHER THAN NOTHING, THAT THE WORLD IS.
THE WORLD IS A COPY OF A PERFECT REALM.
THE WORLD IS A CREATION OF GOD.
THE WORLD IS A MATHEMATICAL HARMONY.

Plato set a precedent when he questioned various aspects of the world around him, rather than focusing on the world itself. From that point on, philosophers have been preoccupied with things of the world, rather than the more primordial fact: the very existence of the world.

Heidegger's philosophy is an attempt to think through the significance of this basic condition of existence which he dubbed...

Being (always capitalized) is that primordial condition or "ground" which allows everything else to come into existence. Heidegger called everything else — people, planets, flowers, jugs—**beings**. Beings (always with a small "b") are those entities which exist in the world. This difficult idea can be better understood through a comparison of Being with light. Without light, human vision would be impossible. Light is a necessary condition for seeing things.

Light

No Light

Likewise, Being is the necessary condition for beings to exist. Without Being, without basic existence, no individual could exist.

Being

No Being

Also, just as one never actually sees light, but rather things lit by light, one never directly experiences Being, but rather beings which exist through Being.

Another approach to understanding Heidegger's idea of Being is to contrast it with what he calls. . . **"The Nothing."** Once we recognize the significance of the world's existence, we can also fathom the possibility of its non-existence. The Nothing is the possibility of the non-existence of all things, literally "no-thing." The notions of Being and the Nothing are difficult to grasp because they are so self-evident that they have been taken for granted.

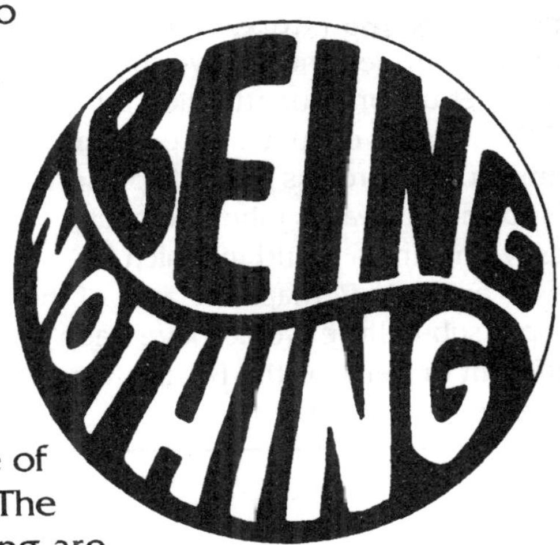

On the other hand, they are central to understanding our condition as humans. To better conceive these ideas, let us turn our attention toward a 20th century cultural figure...**John Lennon**. Regardless of one's personal disposition towards John, we could easily imagine a world in which he never existed. Perhaps the aura of the hippie sub-culture would have been different or perhaps the Beatles would have never existed.

Now think of a world where the Beatles have never existed. Given that they were the first huge international stars of rock and roll, perhaps without their presence rock and roll would never have emerged as the major musical genre it became. From a world where rock and roll never existed, we can continue our line of thought and imagine a world where no music has ever existed.

Each being we eliminate brings us closer and closer to the Nothing.

From the erasure of music, we could fathom the non-existence of all art,

the non-existence of all human practices,

the non-existence of those humans,

the non-existence of the world those humans help constitute,

and finally, the non-existence of the space in which our world revolves.

At that point, we have come to the Nothing, the non-existence of everything. In grasping this possibility of the Nothing, we can appreciate and understand the importance of Being. Being is that which makes all beings possible — the universe, the world, humans, human practices, art, music, rock and roll, the Beatles and John Lennon.

In between these two possibilities, between Being and the Nothing, exist beings. Every entity becomes a being through Being. For example, a "human being" is born into a world of beings.
STATE
Each being, however, is temporal in the sense that time is an intrinsic part of its make-up. Every human being naturally and inevitably grows old. In the end, each being ends up in a state of "nothingness." Every human being eventually dies.

Humans participate in both Being, by existing, and the Nothing, by ceasing to exist. Only the two possibilities of Being and the Nothing are continual.

Heidegger thought that the world we live in, the world of beings, could only be properly understood in light of existence and non-existence, of Being and Nothing.

Due to his insights about existence, Heidegger is considered an important existentialist philosopher. **Existentialism** bases its insight on the fact of primordial existence.

Heidegger, by the way, refused this label for reasons which will be discussed when we examine his relationship to the Existentialist movement in philosophy.

Heidegger thought that the entire history of philosophy, after taking its original cue from Plato, had forgotten about Being and concentrated solely on beings. His exposure of the more primordial Being, he claimed, marked the end of philosophy—a tradition of thinking beings—and started a new task called **"thinking"**—an attempt to understand Being.

Once Heidegger exposed Being, he needed to figure out how to understand its elusive nature. After all, Being is not an individual being, so it is impossible to examine or observe it. He dealt with this concern by examining how the issue of Being arose. How is it possible that Being is an issue? What is it that allows for the asking of questions about Being? His answer:

Similar to the way in which Heidegger exposed the complexity and significance of the self-evident truth that things exist, he showed that because we, as humans, are capable of raising questions about existence and Being, that implies that we, as humans, are somehow capable of *answering* those questions.

We are unique from all other beings because our existence is an issue for us. We, as a special kind of being, can ask those fundamental questions that pertain to every being.

In short, we are capable of inquiring about Being. Human beings are a special type of being, where Being presents itself to be known. Heidegger thought that the ability to raise these issues meant we had a special relationship to them and, somehow, a way of answering them. His explanation of this answer is best understood in relation to the history of philosophy. Past philosophers have always gone about answering important questions by trying to discover some exceptional state of events or exceptional state of mind that could be used to explain the everyday world.

Plato's "theory of ideas" required that one accept reincarnation and otherworldly Forms. Descartes' "thinking thing" presupposed the fantastic assumption that the world did not exist. In fact, each philosopher, in his own way, had ignored the everyday world and gone in search of some extraordinary principle that would explain the world.

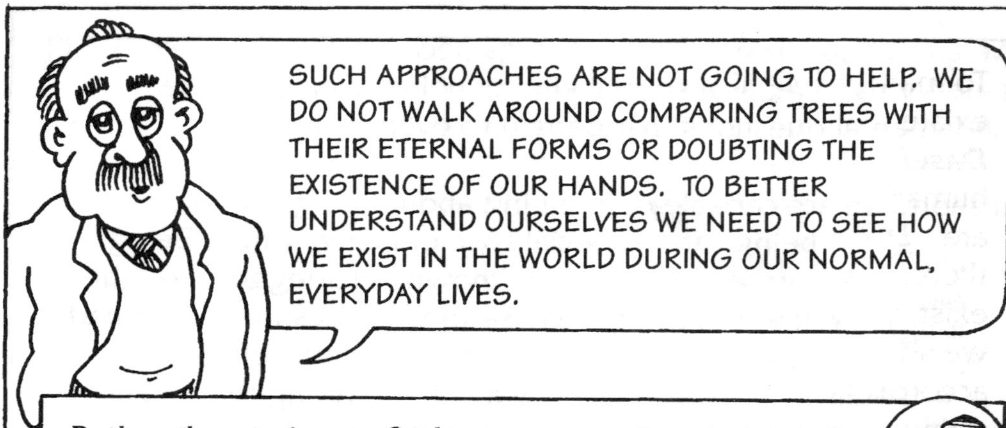

Rather than trying to find some exceptional state of existence, Heidegger decided to do a phenomenological investigation of humans in their **average-everydayness**. (Remember, Husserl's phenomenology is concerned with the "experience" or "awareness" of something.) Simply put, Heidegger investigated the experience of being a typical human being.

As part of his investigation, Heidegger had to figure out the significance of existence for humans, because existence, as the most primordial condition of the world, was bound to affect the entire way humans live.

To mark the significance of our existence, Heidegger gave the name ***Dasein*** to the type of being we call human beings, the type of being you are. *Dasein* translates as "being-there." So before anything else, we exist, we are "there," and that is how we should conceive of ourselves, according to Heidegger, if we are going to understand our lives, our "average-everydayness."

Heidegger turned not only Descartes, but all of the past history of philosophy, on its head. Before Heidegger, it had been thought that one's particular existence had no effect on how one pondered philosophical issues. Consequently, Rousseau, Kant, Nietzsche and even the Zen masters believed they could examine the essence of all humanity.

Heidegger showed how these views ignored a central characteristic of all knowledge with his notion of. . .

THROWN-NESS

Because existence functions as the underlying ground of *Dasein,* our existence determines our possibilities for knowledge (as well as everything else). The event of this existence is our **"thrown-ness."** Basically, the story goes like this...

Heidegger thought that every human (every *Dasein*) is completely shaped by his or her culture. Having no control over the "thrown-ness" of one's social environment, one becomes part of a culture, and **all** of one's behaviors are consequently learned from that culture.

Everything one could possibly do is already proscribed by one's social environment. There is nothing unique about any particular human being. No one is an autonomous individual, free to choose her own way of existing. Heidegger's insight becomes more clear when we examine what he meant by stating that human beings are constituted in terms of their environment.

A child learns how to behave from social interaction with adults. The use of the word "learns," though, is misleading, because it presupposes that there is someone who learns. Adults who interact with the child do not teach, but create behaviors within the child which eventually form what one would call a "person." Only when a newborn has been sufficiently formed by its environment does it become a *Dasein.* These behaviors—moving, thinking, speaking, etc.—which make up our existence, are so basic that we never fully recognize their significance.

Those philosophers who thought they could find a universal essence of humanity did not realize that all practices, including thinking, differ among various cultures and, consequently, that all their "universal systems" only reflected their own particular social environment. There are no intrinsic human natures such as the "will to power" for philosophers to discover. Characteristics we once considered "human nature" are merely characteristics of our particular culture. Heidegger called one's particular culture, the social environment one is thrown into, one's "**world**".

The different social practices of a specific culture make up the "world" of that culture. These shared public "worlds" constitute the standards by which the *Dasein* of a culture act.

In turn, each of these larger worlds can be broken down into smaller ones that more specifically define a *Dasein*. Thus a *Dasein* in America might be involved in...

Depending on the particular world or worlds in which one happens to be involved, certain factors become more or less important in terms of one's constitution. For example, a *Dasein* involved in the world of science might not blink an eye during a stock market crisis. However, a *Dasein* involved in the business world might have a different reaction. *Dasein* is defined by its involvement in various worlds.

To stress the importance of the "world," Heidegger called *Dasein's* activity of existing **being-in-the-world.** The use of the hyphens emphasizes that there is no distance between ourselves and the world. We are as much a part of the world as it is a part of us. Rather than thinking of "in" as a spatial indicator such as being "in" a country or being "in" a box, the easiest way to understand Heidegger's being-in-the-world comes from thinking of "in" as an indicator of involvement such as. . .

Heidegger thought that no distance, either physical or mental, exists between ourselves and our world. Dasein's interest and involvement with its world is intrinsic to Dasein. There is no existing, no "being-there," without a world in which to exist. A person without a world makes no sense. The world and Dasein are one and the same.

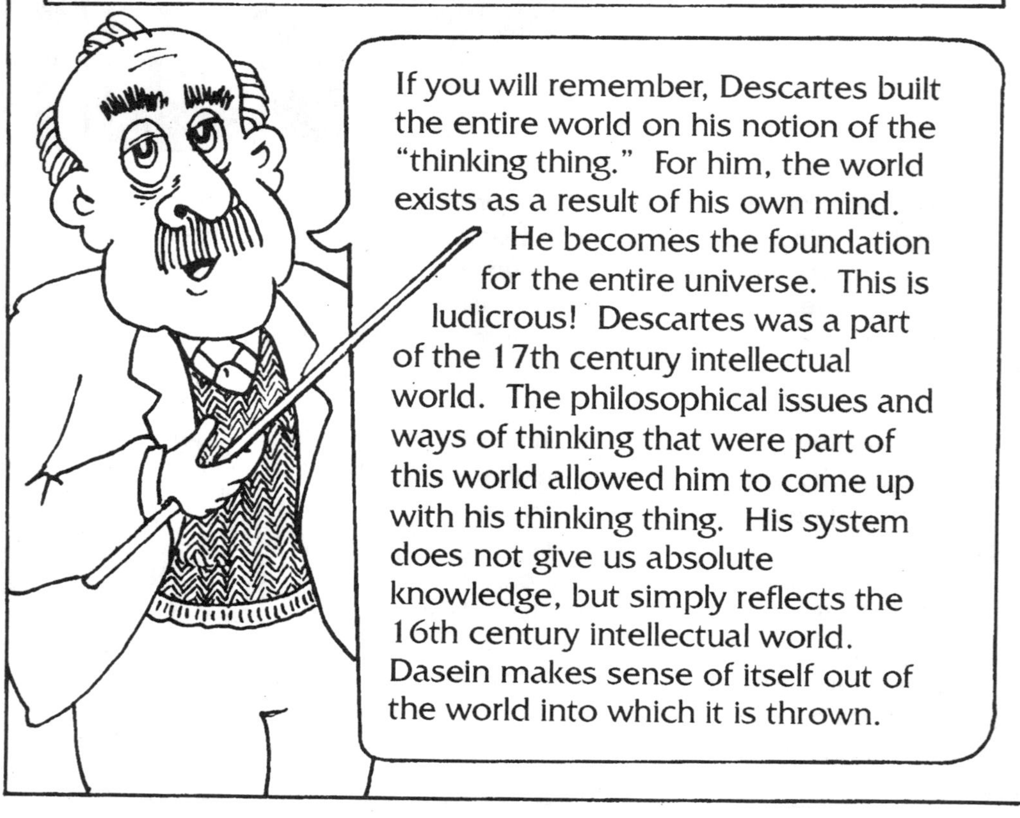

In fact, for Heidegger, there is a very specific way we make sense of our world: through our relationship with. . .

THE ONE

The **One** represents all the possibilities for *Dasein's* world as a collective whole. The One consists of other *Dasein* whose presence creates the world in which an individual *Dasein* can act.

An easier way to understand what Heidegger meant by the One is to imagine how he thought the One functions in our culture.

Heidegger believed that such social practices, which make up *Dasein's* world, are specifically established by the One. The One is the embodiment of a *Dasein's* world and, consequently, of a *Dasein's* personal possibilities — of "what **one** can be." For example, in our culture, one could be a police officer or a doctor or a soldier, but one could not be a witch doctor—the social role does not exist for Westerners. The One has a normative function in the sense that it shapes *Dasein's* behavior.

Heidegger's German term for the One, "das Man," is also translated as "**the They.**"

This translation better illuminates the control and authority the One (or the They) has over each individual.

The One constitutes the environment in which an individual can and must act. It is what gives meaning and intelligibility to each *Dasein's* existence. Through the One, we make sense of ourselves and the world around us by learning how "one lives." Rather than understanding our world through the laws of science or through some god, individuals make the world intelligible by participating in a social context, a world, which has certain customs embodied by and expressed through the One.

Rules for behavior are all just contingent elements of various cultures.
SUNDAY IS A DAY OF REST.
SUNDAY IS A DAY FOR CHURCH.
SUNDAY IS A DAY FOR PLOWING.
All the specific elements of a world each contribute to *Dasein's* most significant activity, being-in-the-world. . .
ALL THESE MANY INGREDIENTS OF "THE ONE"...
...MAKE FOR ONE TASTY LITTLE *DASEIN*.
. . .and being-in-the-world is made sensible in terms of *Dasein's* interaction with the One. The One represents and embodies *Dasein's* world.

In place of an essential human nature, Heidegger stated that each person is constituted by the One. *Dasein* is the One. For a *Dasein* in a particular world, there are three different ways of existing in the world. These ways of existing are something like a mode or attitude a person has toward the world. The simplest way to understand these three types of existence and their accompanying concepts is through example. **So take Carolyn.** Carolyn is thrown into the "world of farming." She grows up on a small peanut plantation down in Georgia, where her parents, grandparents and great grandparents also grew peanuts.

Ever since Carolyn was a young girl, she looked forward to the day when she would take over the family's peanut tradition. Given Carolyn's attitude toward her place in life, Heidegger would say her existence is **undifferentiated**. She has never questioned the meaning of her own life, never recognized her thrown-ness. She has blindly accepted the existence that the One — her family and community— has given to her: the existence of a peanut farmer. Carolyn will live her life unaware and unaffected by the fundamental thrown-ness of her existence.

However, we could imagine Carolyn's life taking a different route. One day as Carolyn is out driving the tractor she has a revelation...

She realizes that her existence as a peanut farmer is a result of sheer coincidence, a result of her thrown-ness. Carolyn decides to change her life, her world.

At this point Carolyn has entered the **inauthentic** mode of existence. Even though she has recognized her thrown-ness, she simply substitutes one life made possible by the One for another. Even though she has entered a new, "military world," all her actions are still part of the One. The form of her life, living as part of the One, remains the same, while the content, her world, has changed.

Going back to the point when Carolyn recognized her thrown-ness, her mode of existence might have become different if her thinking had gone along the following lines: Having recognized the omnipresence of the One, Carolyn began to feel what Heidegger calls **anxiety**.

Upon realizing her thrown-ness, however, a further realization comes to her.

Anxiety is a Dasein's realization that anything they might possibly do has already been defined for them in advance by the One. Eventually, they will return to the Nothing, having lead a life as cogs in the wheel of the One. Anxiety appears when Dasein faces up to the possibility of the Nothing. At this point of realization, Carolyn can do one of two things, the first Heidegger calls **Fallen-ness.**

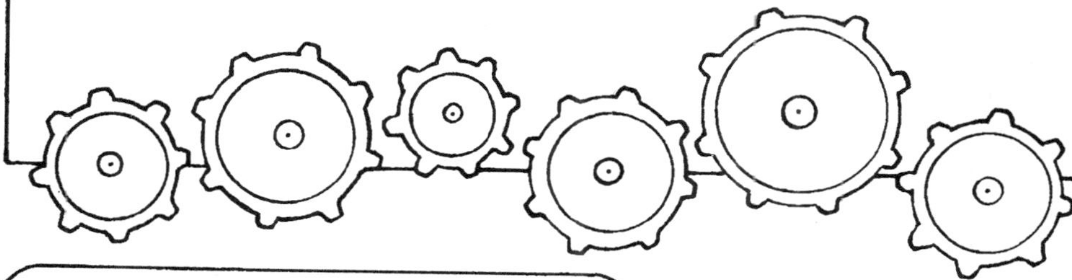

Fallen-ness comes about when Dasein cannot bear the possibility of the Nothing. Instead of dealing with anxiety, a Dasein refuses to recognize the situation at hand and immerses itself back into the world of the One, once again becoming inauthentic.

Carolyn's second option is to face up to the Nothing.

At this point Carolyn becomes a **being-toward-death.** While all ways of life are defined by the One, every Dasein has to face the Nothing—has to die—on its own. Death becomes Dasein's most unique possibility. Once this is realized, Dasein's entire relationship with the world is transformed.

Given that Dasein, not the One, is responsible for its own death, Dasein, not the One, also becomes responsible for its own life. Heidegger calls this transformation **care.** In caring for its world, Dasein makes the most of its own possibilities—even if those possibilities were originally defined by the One. . .

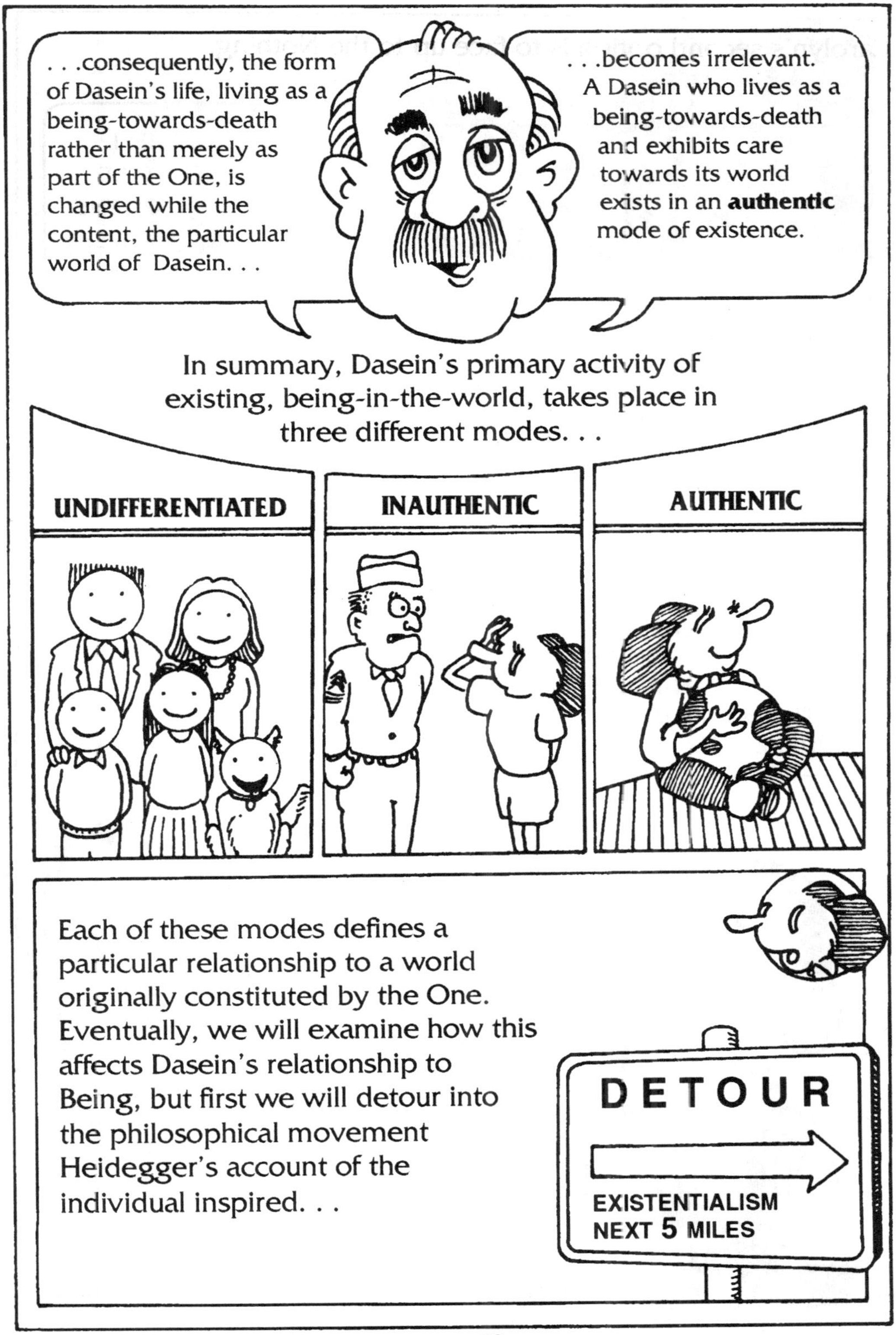
. . .consequently, the form of Dasein's life, living as a being-towards-death rather than merely as part of the One, is changed while the content, the particular world of Dasein. . .
. . .becomes irrelevant. A Dasein who lives as a being-towards-death and exhibits care towards its world exists in an **authentic** mode of existence.
In summary, Dasein's primary activity of existing, being-in-the-world, takes place in three different modes. . .
UNDIFFERENTIATED
INAUTHENTIC
AUTHENTIC
Each of these modes defines a particular relationship to a world originally constituted by the One. Eventually, we will examine how this affects Dasein's relationship to Being, but first we will detour into the philosophical movement Heidegger's account of the individual inspired. . .
DETOUR
EXISTENTIALISM NEXT 5 MILES

existentialism

Existentialism takes its starting point from the brute fact of existence. The existentialist philosophers considered the human situation absurd. Without any timeless truth, not much matters. Despite the fact that, for them, the world is meaningless, they firmly believed in the individual's responsibility for their actions.

Absurdity also means recognizing that the world is not, in fact, ordered the way we conceive of it. For the existentialists, we filter the world through language, in a manner similar to Kant's categories, which fosters a particular experience of the world.

Absurdity is recognizing the world without the concepts we posit upon it. This is the experience—horrifying to some existentialists, liberating to others—of meaninglessness.

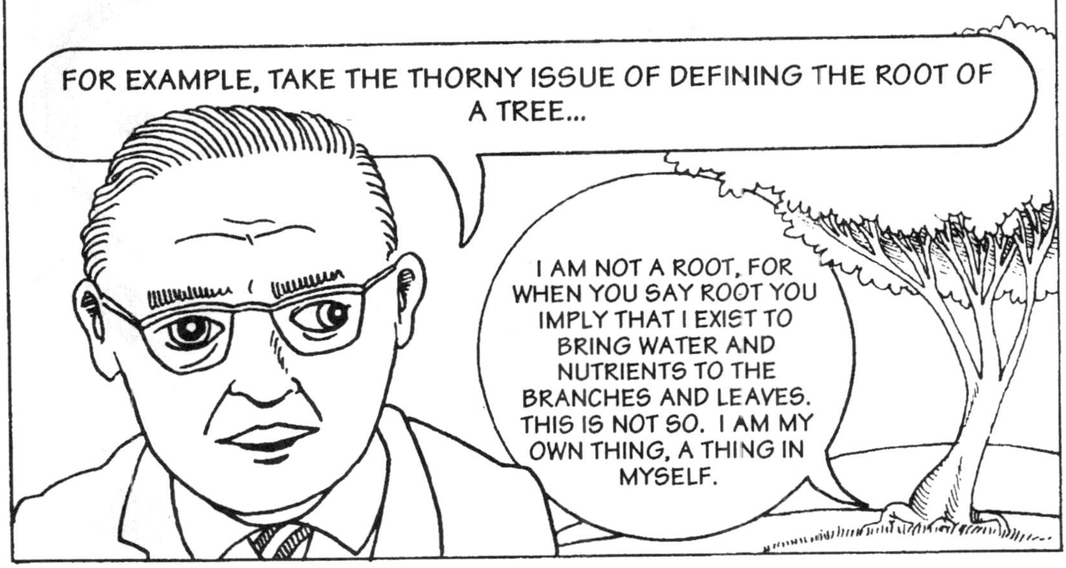

This recognition of meaninglessness has great consequences for the individual. The most important existentialist philosopher, Jean-Paul Sartre, thought that the meaninglessness of existence made the individual radically free.
LIVING IN A WORLD WITHOUT MEANING IMPLIES THAT THERE IS NO JUSTIFICATION FOR AN INDIVIDUAL'S LIFE, DESPITE WHAT ANY PARTICULAR INDIVIDUAL MIGHT BELIEVE. SINCE THE WORLD IS MEANINGLESS, THERE IS NO REASON TO CHOOSE ONE WAY OF LIFE OVER ANOTHER. CONSEQUENTLY, WE ARE FREE TO CHOOSE ANY TYPE OF EXISTENCE, BECAUSE NO ONE WAY HOLDS ANY PRIORITY OVER ANY OTHER.
THANKS, I FEEL A LOT BETTER...LOOK OUT BELOW!

SO YOU'RE SAYING MY LIFE IS MEANINGLESS?
ABSOLUTELY!
BUT WHAT'S THE POINT OF IT ALL THEN?
THAT'S EXACTLY IT! THERE IS NONE! WELCOME TO YOUR FREEDOM!

One of the main points of existentialism is Sartre's idea that "existence precedes essence." This is similar to Heidegger's insight that a person is, first and foremost, a product of their world. But for Sartre, this simply means that humans have no pregiven nature. While Heidegger thought that the individual was merely part of his environment, part of the One, Sartre drew the opposite conclusion: that each individual was an autonomous self.

RATHER THAN THE SELF DESCARTES THOUGHT YOU ALL HAD, THE "THINKING THING", YOUR SELF IS NOT SOME PREGIVEN THING, BUT A COLLECTION OF FRAGMENTS. THE SELF IS A CONSTANTLY CHANGING CONGLOMERATION OF ONE'S ACTIONS. THEREFORE, YOUR ACTIONS DO NOT COME FROM YOUR SELF, BUT YOUR SELF COMES FROM YOUR ACTIONS.

SARTRE HELD ABSOLUTE VIGILANCE OVER THE IDEA THAT THE INDIVIDUAL IS FREE TO CHOOSE THESE ACTIONS. FOR SARTRE, ONE CANNOT ATTRIBUTE ONE'S ACTIONS TO ONE'S PSYCHOLOGY OR SITUATION. ONE IS FREE TO CHOOSE HOW TO ACT, OR IF TO ACT AT ALL. SARTRE THOUGHT THAT PEOPLE WHO DENIED THEIR FREEDOM WERE LIVING IN BAD FAITH.

Admitting the meaninglessness of one's existence and accepting responsibility for all of one's actions is what Sartre called **authenticity.** For Sartre, this meant that one embraced one's freedom. With no God and no meaning to explain existence, everything that you are results from what you have done, and for this accumulation, you alone are responsible.

It was over this existentialist preoccupation with the self, among other things, that caused Heidegger to reject the entire movement.
I GUESS MARTIN'S NOT SHOWING UP...
THAT'S DEFINITELY NOT ME...
Heidegger saw existentialism as just another version of Descartes' philosophy. The self of existentialism was basically the same as the thinking thing: Each view centered the entire world around the individual. . .

. . .consequently, the existentialists made the same mistake as the other philosophers by focusing all their attention on one type of being and forgetting about that which makes beings possible. . .

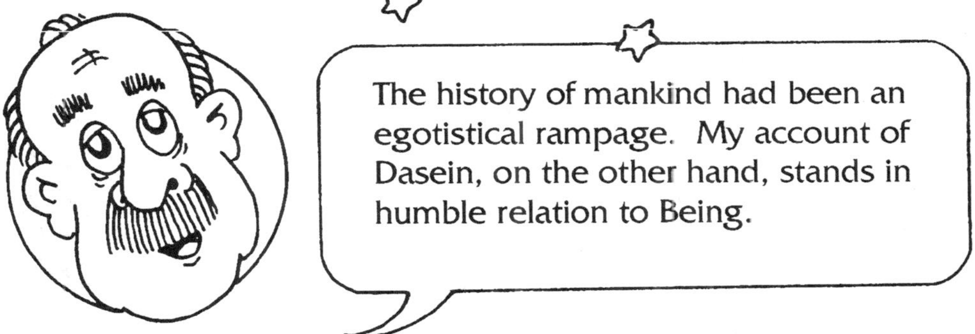

Not only, according to Heidegger, was it incorrect to center philosophy solely around one particular being, the historical focus of philosophy on humanity has caused the crisis of the modern world!

In order to understand the connection between human-centered philosophy and our global problems, we need to examine Heidegger's critique of Descartes as representative of this historico-philosophical prejudice.

For Heidegger, Descartes' "thinking thing" symbolizes all the metaphors we use to think about ourselves as individuals. Notions such as. . .

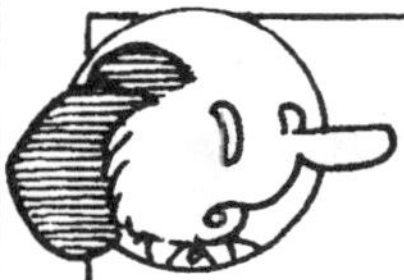

...which all give rise to an egotistical way of thinking. By looking at ourselves as some sort of "thinking thing", we implicitly place ourselves, both individually and collectively, at the center of the world. To put it bluntly, everything exists for us. Or. . .

Rather than recognizing our place within the world, our status as one being among all other beings, we have turned the world into something which exists for and because of the "thinking thing."

This way of existing, looking at the world in terms of the "thinking thing," Heidegger calls. . .

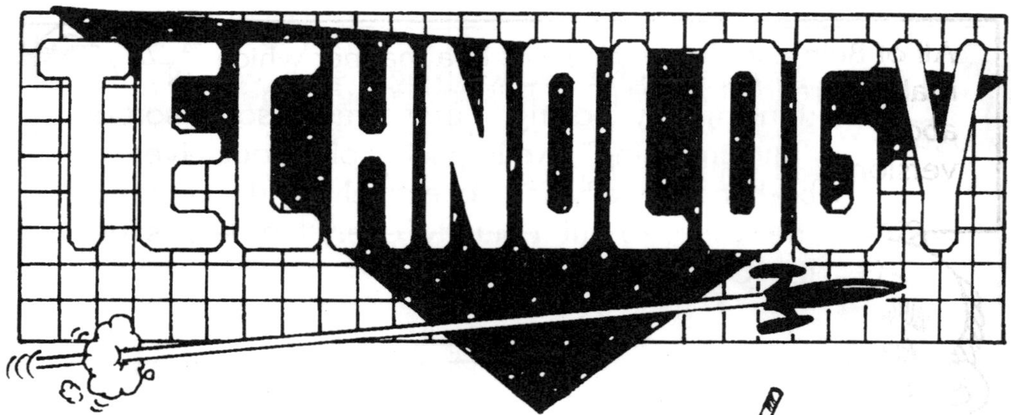

But technology, in this sense, does not refer to our everyday understanding of the world but rather to a specific way of seeing the world, an attitude which reveals everything in the world to us in a certain way. All the beings in the world, everything around us, are seen as something there for us to consume. The entire world becomes "stuff" which exists exclusively for our purposes.

The word Heidegger uses to describe beings once they have been transformed by technology into "stuff" is. . .

bestand

Translated into English, *bestand* means "standing reserve" or "stock."

All of Being, as *bestand,* exists in a manner which makes it ready for our use. This revealing comes about when we think about ourselves as some version of the "thinking thing."

Take, for instance, the contemplation of a tree.

ITS LEAVES TAKE IN CARBON-DIOXIDE AND GIVE OFF OXYGEN, SO WE CAN BREATHE. THE ROOTS PREVENT EROSION AND HOLD THE LAND IN PLACE IN ORDER TO MAKE THE LAND INHABITABLE.
IT SUPPLIES THE MATERIAL WHICH BUILT OUR COUNTRY AND STILL SUPPLIES THE PAPER WHICH KEEPS IT MOVING.

When we think of ourselves as the existence-giving "thinking thing," as we have for the last four hundred years, all the world becomes something for our use. We cannot fathom the tree without somehow seeing it as existing for us.

Trees, as well as everything else, have no value independent from the value we give them. Rather than seeing the world as filled with other beings, each having their own independent existence, we see it as "stock" existing for the exclusive use of the thinking

So technology, in the normal sense of the word, is just one small part of the technological attitude, an attitude which arises as a result of seeing humanity as the center of the universe.
Heidegger calls this technological attitude ***gestell,*** which translates as "framing." The use of framing designates this attitude which divides up stock, or enframes it, for use. This process, if it would have happened systematically rather than piecemeal, would go as follows:

In the beginning, there existed the entire world of beings which functioned harmoniously under Being.
However, human beings, taking up the technological attitude of the thinking thing, framed the world and turned it into stock in order to make it more accessible for use.
The whole was split up, or enframed, for humanity's convenience. "Land" was sharply delineated from "water."
LEAVE ME OUT OF THIS.
This land was then given sharp boundaries which do not exist naturally—first "continents," then "countries," then "states," then "communities."

After the "land" was sectioned off into small consumable bits, humanity framed off all the beings that existed on those sections for their own use. The land and its inhabitancy were then used for the purpose of one specific being, Dasein.
Heidegger felt that all these abuses of nature arose from the technological attitude we bring to the world. If the world exists because of humanity, then there is nothing humanity cannot do to it or with it.
THE WORLD IS LIKE PUTTY IN OUR HANDS.

In fact, it is easy to see how culturally relative and dangerous our self-concepts are when we apply Heidegger's views to our interactions with non-Western cultures—cultures the West has been racist enough to consider non-"thinking things."

The world exists to be used. It exists for those thinking things who have the power to exploit it.

Due to the prevalent technological attitude, many of the world's atrocities can be traced back to this supposedly harmless philosophical belief that we are somehow individuals providing reference for the world, that we are somehow a version of the "thinking thing." Seeing ourselves like this, we lose respect for all the other beings in the world, lose our recognition of Being itself.

For Heidegger, any way of looking at the world which focuses exclusively on one type of being (which would include the way most philosophers have approached things) precludes the possibility of seeing the world in a multitude of ways — appreciative, respectful, artistic.

Only by realizing that humanity is one being among many and merely part of an all-encompassing Being can we begin to live in harmony with the rest of the world.

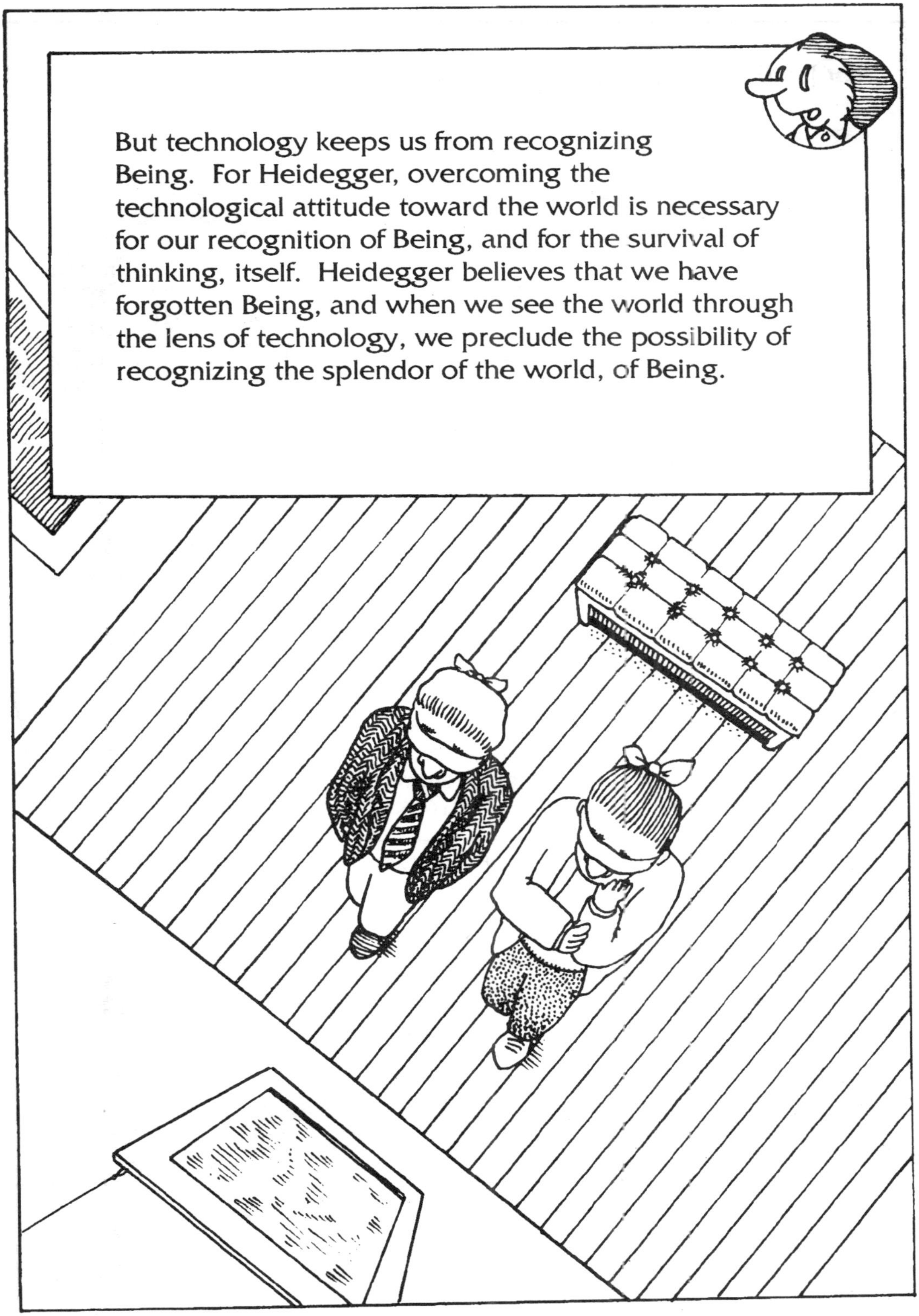
But technology keeps us from recognizing Being. For Heidegger, overcoming the technological attitude toward the world is necessary for our recognition of Being, and for the survival of thinking, itself. Heidegger believes that we have forgotten Being, and when we see the world through the lens of technology, we preclude the possibility of recognizing the splendor of the world, of Being.

For Heidegger. . .with a technological attitude, we separate beings from their primordial contexts.

This brings us back to the notion of care, which allows us to live authentically. Heidegger thinks that care provides an alternative to the technological attitude. When we care for an individual being, we care for it as part of Being as a whole. We recognize all the other things in harmony with that individual being.

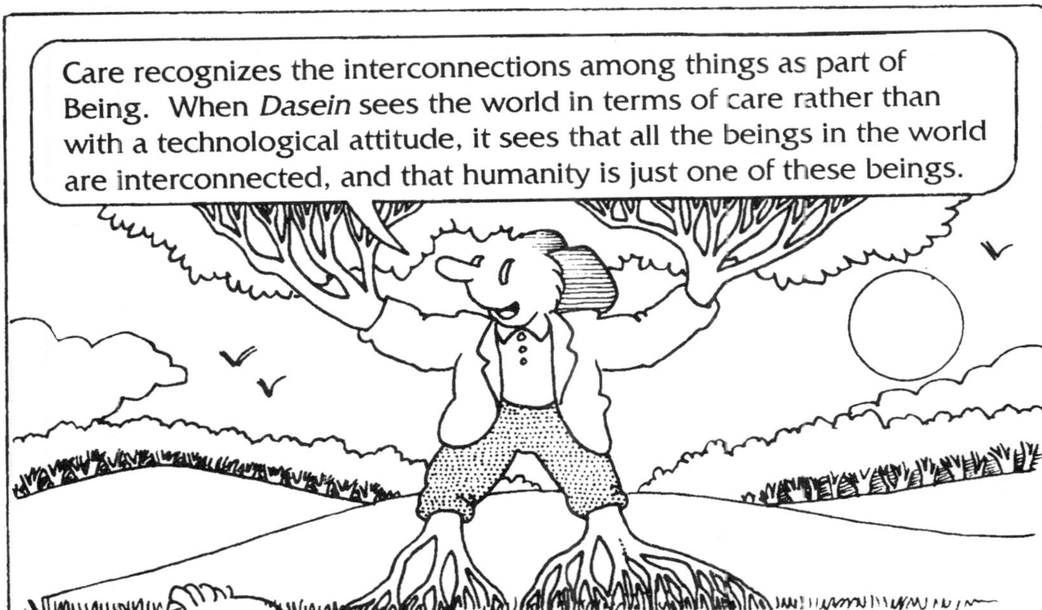

For Heidegger, art is a way of appreciating the interconnections among beings that technology ignores. Art is opposed to technology, because it does not treat beings as standing reserve, homogenous "stuff" waiting for our use.

Consider a pair of peasant shoes:

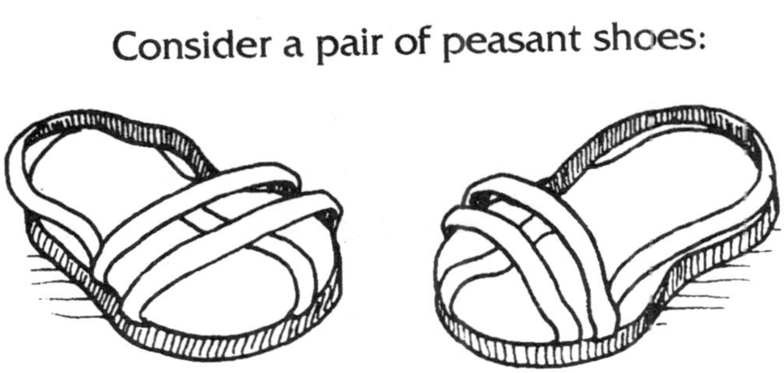

From a technological viewpoint, these shoes are just objects, just "stuff." They can be measured, torn apart, and made into something else, or given a monetary worth.

But an artistic attitude toward the shoes, rather than a technological one, yields a different kind of appreciation. .

Vincent Van Gogh's **"A Pair of Shoes"** (1886).

BUT FOR ME THESE SHOES ARE DIFFERENT. I SHOW THE SHOES IN THEIR CONTEXT. MY PAINTING SHOWS THAT THEY ARE NOT JUST OBJECTS, BUT A PART OF SOMEBODY'S WORLD. THEY HAVE A HISTORY, AND TO SOMEBODY THEY ARE VERY IMPORTANT.

SOMEONE WALKS FOR MILES IN THESE SHOES EVERY DAY, AND COMES HOME EXHAUSTED IN THEM AT NIGHT. SOMEONE LIVES AND WORKS IN THEM, AND EVERY SCRATCH AND TATTER IS AN EVIDENCE OF SOMEONE'S WHOLE EXISTENCE, THE ENTIRE WORLD OF A PEASANT FARMER.

In Van Gogh's painting we experience the meaning of the shoes. In the work of art, the truth of Being is at work.

By contrasting art to technology, Heidegger wants to show us that there are different ways of being-in-the-world. Some of them, like art, involve a caring for things in their contexts and with their historical significance. This is a part of living authentically. But other ways, like technological ones, which treat everything as standing reserve, deny that we are one being among many beings. . .and, consequently, deny Being itself.

How do we attain such a relationship with the world? How do we attain an attitude that is not technological? By recognizing ourselves as Dasein and not the thinking thing, we are in a position to realize that a certain social practice we have allows us to recognize our relationship to Being and, in turn, shows us how to live in response to that relationship. This practice, the central preoccupation of the latter part of Heidegger's life, is...

LANGUAGE

Through our language we have a way of experiencing our original relationship with the mystery of existence.
Language is something like an extended memory for Being, which records all the moments when beings come into existence.
Every historical appearance of Being creates a special word which then becomes a symbol of that appearance.
If we trace our most fundamental words back to their origins, we can recall the original experience of their coming into existence through Being.

The following example helps illustrate the primordial significance Heidegger gave to language. Take the word "love" as it is used today in our society.

After seeing the word "Love" used on thousands of greeting cards, soap commercials, movie reviews and tie-dye tee shirts, the word has become impoverished. "Love" no longer carries the meaning and significance it once did. Today, saying "I love you" is not much different from saying "Pass the salt."

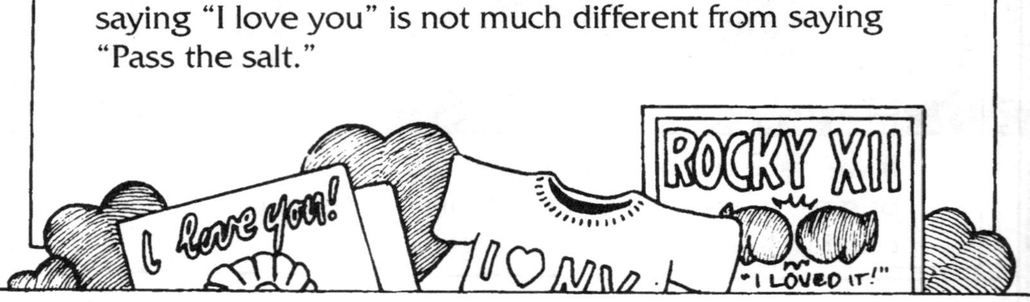

Heidegger thought that this process of words becoming impoverished took place over a long period of time. Each generation adds another layer of crud over the original meaning of a word, covering it like layers of rust. To follow Heidegger's view, there was a moment in time when someone first used the word "love."

At this moment there was no difference between the word and its meaning, between the word and the untainted experience of it. "Love" came into existence at the moment it was spoken. In that very instant, the being called "love" came into existence through Being.

"i love you"

For Heidegger, the key to understanding our place in the world comes from recognizing the initial moment of existence, the moment "Being speaks," that lies at the center of our most important words. By uncovering all the layers of rust that history has placed over the original experience of the words central to our lives—truth, knowledge, human, etc.,—we can once again live in regard to these events of existence.

So, for example, when someone says, **"I love you,"** they will experience the true and original significance of their words and, consequently, act in a manner which accepts the responsibility for such an utterance.

The original experience of most of the words central to our lives are embedded in the Greek language. According to Heidegger, the Greek language is no ordinary language but rather one with a special and immanent relationship to Being.

Our fundamental words come into existence through Being in the Greek language, a language in which those fundamental questions were first voiced. Due to the language's special relationship to beings and Being, Heidegger stated that Greek was the ***Logos:*** a language where the words of the language are inseparable from what they name.

In order to uncover and experience our most important words, we have to trace them back to their original existence in Greek. Once we have done this, we can begin to understand our relationship with Being.

Our entire language, the language of *Dasein*, becomes the living memory of beings coming into existence or, as Heidegger put it, **"Language is the house of Being."** We are that special being who can ask questions about Being and, having that ability, we become the keepers or guardians of Being.

2000 years of egotistical philosophical assumptions have obscured our unique relationship to Being.

Forgetting
the most important
characteristic of our existence has cost a severe
price, the price of a world dominated by
the technological
attitude.

Heidegger did not only give us a new philosophy, he gave us a new way of understanding what it means to exist, what it means ***to be.***
Heidegger's BE-Spectacle Shoppe
I'M SIMPLY BEDAZZLED!

Towards the end of his life, Heidegger wrote on what it means for a human to live a life in regard to Being. He called this existence **dwelling.** When one dwells upon the earth, one lives a poetic life as an attendant of Being.

Living in light of the fundamental mystery of existence, Heidegger felt, was something that could not be explained, only experienced. For a catalyst to that experience, one must turn to Heidegger's writings. Perhaps through them the mystery of Being might be revealed.

Heidegger's work has been the inspiration for some of the greatest thinkers of the 20th century...
"My **deconstruction** of Western philosophy has been considered some of the most radical thought in history." **Jacques Derrida** (born 1930)
"By doing an **archaeology** of knowledge, I have exposed the shaky foundations upon which most of the social sciences are built." **Michel Foucault** (1926-1984)
"I account for the unconscious without recourse to a self." **Hans Georg Gadamer** (born 1900)
"My work, **hermeneutics,** is the understanding of understanding." **Jacques Lacan** (1901-1981)
Besides his influence in philosophy and psychoanalysis, Heidegger's work has helped shape new ways of thinking in aesthetics, theology, cultural studies and literary criticism.

Despite his monumental influence, contemporary opinion of Heidegger is radically ambivalent. While many philosophers extol Heidegger as one of the central figures in the history of Western thought, other respected thinkers do not consider him a serious philosopher at all, but rather a mystic or meta-theologian.

Until enough time passes for these diverse views to settle, it seems the best we can hope for is the courage to engage with a thinker who might offer a new, non-technological way of existing, a new way to be.

HEIDEGGER AND NAZISM

Heidegger was a member of the Nazi party until the end of World War II. His involvement with the party and his support of its world view are undisputed. Even more disturbing than his active participation in Nazism, Heidegger never attempted to account for his support of the Nazis outside of calling his involvement with them "a blunder." In this light, Heidegger stands as a great embarrassment for philosophers. The key focus of recent years, however, has been to decide whether or not his philosophy somehow reflects his political ideology, to see if Being and Nazism are somehow related. The most evident place that supports a connection is his account of human beings.

If humans are *Dasein*, meaning they have no common essence, then there is no reason to expect that a particular group of *Dasein* will respect the rights of another. The only sense of security a *Dasein* has comes from their given society. Consequently, Heidegger's account of *Dasein* can lead to absolute nationalism. "I'm a German, and you're not; therefore you are a threat." Here we see how such a view easily lent itself to the Nazi platform, which stated that Germans are a unique race, a superior people. This political reading of *Dasein*, as well as many other keen insights into Heidegger's philosophy, are explained in Richard Wolin's *The Politics of Being* (Columbia University Press, 1990).

Heidegger was a nasty character or, as one prominent American philosopher put it, a German redneck. At this point, we can only wait to see if Heidegger the philosopher can be rescued from Heidegger the political figure.

"THE WORLD IS DARKENING."

Martin Heidegger

THE END

FURTHER READING

The best introduction to Heidegger's philosophy is in a book written by George Steiner called *Martin Heidegger* (University of Chicago Press, 1978). In it, Steiner gives a clear account of Heidegger's many writings. As far as reading the man himself, the most representative book available is a collection of essays called *Basic Writings* (Harper & Collins, 1993), which is edited by David Farrell Krell. The book includes the introduction to *Being and Time* and nine essays covering such topics as metaphysics, truth, art, mathematics, modern science, technology, dwelling and thinking. For an overall placement of Heidegger's views in modern philosophy as well as an account of Sartre and other existentialists, Robert C. Solomon's *Continental Philosophy Since 1750* (Oxford University Press, 1988) does an excellent job of contextualizing Heidegger within the European philosophical tradition.

Heidegger's Works Available in English

The following list is a sampling of Martin Heidegger's works available in English translation in book form. It is not a complete inventory.

A catalogue of Heidegger's works, along with a thorough survey of the secondary literature can be found in Hans-Martin Sass, *Heidegger-Bibliographie* (Meisenheim am Glan: Anton Hain Verlag, 1968), supplemented by Hans-Martin *Sass et al., Materialen zur Heidegger-Bibliographie 1917-1972* (Meisenheim am Glan: Anton Hain Verlag, 1975).

The bibliography best suited to students' needs belongs to perhaps the finest introductory work on Heidegger's thought: Walter Biemel, *Heidegger* (Reinbek bei Hamburg: Rowohlt Taschenbuch Verlag, 1973), available in an English translation by J.L. Mehta (New York: Harcourt Brace Jovanovich, 1976).

Among the works by Martin Heidegger available in English are:

Being and Time. Translated by John Macquarrie and Edward Robinson. New York: Harper & Row, 1962. (*Sein und Zeit, 1927.)*

Early Greek Thinking. Translated by David Farrell Krell and Frank A. Capuzzi. New York: Harper & Row, 1975. (Der Sprach des Anaximander" from *Holzwege,* 1950, pp. 296-343; "Logos (Heraklit, Fragment B 50)," "Moira (Parmenides VIII, 34-41)," and "Aietheia (Heraklit, Fragment B 16)" from *Vortrage und Auf sätze,* 1954, pp. 207-282.

The End of Philosophy. Translated by Joan Stambaugh. New York Harper & Row, 1973. ("Die Metaphysik als Geschichte des Seins "Entwürfe zur Geschichte des Seins als Metaphysik," and "De Erinnerung in die Metaphysik" from *Nietzsche,* 1961, vol. II, pp. 399-490; "Oberwindung der Metaphysik" from *Vorträge und Aufsätze,* 1954, pp. 71-99.)

The Essence of Reasons. A bilingual edition. Translation by Terence Malick, Evanston, Illinois: Northwestern University Press, 1969. (*Vom Wesen des Grundes,* 1929.)

Existence and Being. Edited, with introduction, by Werner Brock, Chicago: Henry Regnery Company, 1949. (In addition to other translation of Readings II and III in this anthology, the volume contains translations of "Heimkunft: An die Verwandten" and "Hölderlin und das Wesen der Dichtung" from *Erläuterungen Zu Hölderlius Dichtung,* 1951, pp. 9-45.)

Hegel's Concept of Experience Translated by J. Glenn Gray and Fred D. Wieck. New York: Harper & Row, 1970. ("Hegels Begriff der Erfahrung," *Holzwege,* 1950, pp. 105-192.)

Identity and Difference. A bilingual edition. Translation by Joan Stambaugh. New York: Harper & Row, 1969. (*Identitat und Differenz,* 1957.)

An Introduction to Metaphysics. Translated by Ralph Manheim. Garden City, New York: Doubleday-Anchor Books, 1961. (*Einführung in die Metaphysik,* 1953.)

Kant and the Problem of Metaphysics. Translated by James S. Churchill. Bloomington, Indiana: Indiana University Press, 1962. (*Kant und das Problem der Metaphysik,* 1929.)

Nietzsche Four volumes. Edited by David Farrell Krell. New York: Harper & Row, forthcoming. (*Nietzsche,* 2 vols., 1961.)

On the Way to Language. Translated by Peter D. Hertz and Joan Stambaugh. New York: Harper & Row, 1971. (*Unterwegs zur Sprache,* 1959. The English edition does not follow the sequence of the essays in the German edition and omits the first essay—which appears in *Poetry, Language, Thought,* listed below.)

On Time and Being Translated by Joan Stambaugh. New York: Harper & Row, 1972. (*Zur Sache des Denkens,* 1969.)

Poetry, Language, Thought. Translated by Albert Hofstadter. New York: Harper & Row, 1971. (*Aus der Erfahrung des Denkens,* 1954; *Der Ursprung des Kunstwekes* (Reclam), 1960: "Wozu Dichter?" from *Holzwege, 1950,* pp. 248-295; "Bauen Wohnen Denken," "Das Ding," and "...Dichterisch wohnet der Mensch...." from *Vorträge und Aufsätze,* 1954, pp. 145-204-; "Die Sprache" from *Unterwegs zur Sprache,* 1959, pp. 9-33.)

The Question Concerning Technology and Other Essays. Translated by William Lovitt. New York: Harper & Row. ("Die Frage nach der Technik" and "Wissenschaft und Besinnung" from *Vorträge und Arefscitze,* 1954, pp. 13-70; "Die Zeit des Welkbildes" and "Nietzsches Wort 'Gott ist tot'" from *Holzwege,* 1950, pp. 69-104 and 193-247.)

The Question of Being A bilingual edition. Translation by William Kluback and Jean T. Wilde. New Haven, Connecticut: College & University Press, 1958. (*Zur Seinsfrage,* 1956.)

What Is a Thing? Translated by W.B. Barton, Jr. and Vera Deutsch. Chicago: Henry Regnery Company, 1967. (*Die Frage nach dem Ding,* 1962.)

What Is Called Thinking? Translated by Fred D. Wieck and J. Glenn Gray. New York: Harper & Row, 1968. (*Was heisst Denken?* 1954.)

What Is Philosophy? A bilingual edition. Translation by William Kluback and Jean T. Wilde, New Haven, Connecticut: College & University Press, 1958. (*Was ist das—die Philosophie?* 1956.)

Martin Heidegger: In His Own Words

On the History of Philosophy:

On the basis of the Greeks' initial contributions towards an Interpretation of Being, a dogma has been developed which not only declares the question about the meaning of Being to be superfluous, but sanctions its complete neglect.

On the Essence of Truth:

Absolute mystery, mystery as such, pervades the whole of man's Dasein...He is the more mistaken the more he exclusively takes himself as the measure of all things.

On the Subject:

Man is never primarily this side of the world as a "subject," whether in the sense of an "I" or a "we." Nor is he primarily and exclusively a subject and always in relationship to an object so that his nature is to be seen in a subject-object relation. Man, in his nature, ec-sists rather primarily into the openness of Being, and it is this openness which illumines and clears the "between" where it is possible for a subject-object "relationship" to "be."

On Being:

All being is in Being. To put it more pointedly, being *is* Being.

On the "Nothing":

Only because Nothing is revealed in the very basis of our *Dasein* is it possible for the utter strangeness of what-is to dawn on us. Only when the strangeness of what-is forces itself upon us does it awaken and invite our wonder. Only because of wonder, that is to say, the revelation of the Nothing, does the "Why?" spring to our lips. Only because this "Why?" is possible as such can we seek for reasons and proofs in a definite way. Only because we can ask and prove are we fated to become esquires in this life.

On Existence:

The most primordial, and indeed the most authentic, disclosedness, in which Dasein as a potentiality-for-Being, can be, is the *truth of existence.*

On "Dasein":

To work out the question of Being adequately, we must make an entity—the inquirer—the transparent in his own Being. The very asking of this question is an entity's mode of *Being*; and as such it gets its essential character from what is inquired about—namely, Being. This entity which each of us is himself and which includes inquiring as one of the possibilities of its Being, we shall denote by the term "Dasein" (being-there).

On "Thrownness":

This characteristic of Dasein's being—that "that it is"—is veiled in its "whence" and "whither," yet disclosed in itself all the more unveiledly; we call it the "*thrownness*" of this entity into its "there."

On "being-in-the-world":

Dasein is that entity which is characterized as being-in-the-world. Human life is not some subject that has to perform some trick in order to enter the world. Dasein as being-in-the-world means: being in the world in such a way that this Being means: dealing with the world.

On the "One" (the "They"):

Dasein's everyday possibilities of Being are for the Others to dispose of as they please. These Others, moreover, are not *definite* Others. On the contrary, any Other can represent them. What is decisive is just that inconspicuous domination by Others which has already been taken over unawares from Dasein as Being-with. One belongs to the Others oneself and enhances their power...The "who" is not this one, not that one, not oneself, not some people, and not the sum of them all. The who is the neuter, *the "they."*

On Anxiety:

Anxiety throws Dasein back upon that which it is anxious about - its authentic potentiality-for-Being-in-the-world. Anxiety individualizes Dasein for its own most Being in the world, which as something that understands, projects itself essentially upon possibilities.

On Death:

No one can take the other's dying away from him...By its very essence, death is in every case mine, in so far as it "is" at all. And indeed death signifies a peculiar possibility-of-Being in which the very Being of one's own Dasein is an issue. In dying, it is shown that mineness and existence are ontologically constitutive for death. Dying is not an event; it is a phenomenon to be understood existentially.

On Authentic Existence:

Proximally Dasein is "they," and for the most part it remains so. If Dasein discovers the world in its own way and brings it close, if it discloses to itself its own authentic being, then this discovery of the world and this disclosure of Dasein are always accomplished as a clearing away of concealments and obscurities, as a breaking up of the disguises with which Dasein bars its own way.

On Technology:

The coming to presence of technology threatens revealing, threatens it with the possibility that all revealing will be consumed in ordering and that everything will present itself only in the unconcealedness of standing-reserve. Human activity can never directly counter this danger. Human achievement alone can never banish it. But human reflection can ponder the fact that all saving power must be of a higher essence than what is endangered, though at the same time kindred to it.

On National Socialism:

The works that are being peddled about nowadays as the philosophy of National Socialism but have nothing whatever to do with inner truth and greatness of this movement (namely the encounter between global technology and modern man) - have all been written by men fishing in the troubled waters of "values" and "totalities."

On Our Modern World:

The darkening of the world, the flight of the gods, the destruction of the earth, the transformation of men into a mass, the hatred and suspicion of everything free and creative, have assumed such proportions throughout the earth that such childish categories as pessimism and optimism have long since become absurd.

Index

absolute axiom (Cartesian), 13-16
absurdity, 60-61
anamnesis, 9-11
anxiety, 56-57
archaeology (Foucault), 99
art, 83-85
authenticity, 59, 67, 82
average-everydayness, 42-43

bad faith, 66-67
Beauvoir, Simone de, 60
Being, 33-40, 69, 80-81, 91
  and words, 87-93
Being and Time (Heidegger), 30
being-in-the-world, 47-48, 52-59, 85
beings, 34
  human, 38-43
being-toward-death, 58-59
Berkeley, George, 17
Bestand (stock, stuff), 72-73, 75, 83-84

Camus, Albert, 60
care, 58-59, 82-83
categorical imperative, 20
child-raising, 44-45
Christianity, 22, 26
culture, human, 44-46, 49-53, 64
cultures, Non-Western, 79

Dasein, 43-59, 69, 102
death, 57-59
deconstruction, 99
Derrida, Jacques, 99
Descartes, René, 5, 13-16, 41, 43, 48, 65, 68, 70-71
dreams, 14-15

Duns Scotus, 28
dwelling (Heidegger), 97

empiricists, 18
ethics, 20, 23
evil demon, 15, 16
existence, 31-33
  authentic, 59, 67, 82
  inauthentic, 55, 57, 59
  undifferentiated, 54, 59
existentialism, 39, 60-69
experience, everyday, 27, 42-43

faith, 25-26
  bad, 66-67
  leap of, 25
fallen-ness, 57
forms (Platonic), 8-11
Foucault, Michel, 99
freedom, existential, 62-67
Freiburg, University of, 29-30

Gadamer, Hans Georg, 99
geometry, 24
gestell (framing), 76-78
God:
  death of, 25
  existence of, 16, 22, 25
Greeks:
  language, 92-93
  philosophers, ancient, 5-12

Heidegger, Martin:
  critics of, 100, 102-3
  influence of, 99-101
  life history, 29-31, 102
  quoted, 1, 3, 104
  reaction to other philosophers, 28, 69-70
  writings of, 30, 98, 103

Heraclitus, 7
hermeneutics (Lacan), 99
human nature, effect of culture on, 44-46, 49-53, 64
humans:
as beings, 38-43
as Dasein, 43-59, 69, 102
own belief in centrality of, 1-5
as thinking animals, 4-5, 16, 40- 41, 48, 65, 68, 70-71, 73-75, 79
Hume, David, 17
Husserl, Edmund, 26-27, 29, 42

idealism, 17
Ideas (Platonic), 8-11, 41
infinity, 25

Kant, Immanuel, 18-20, 43, 61
Kierkegaard, Soren, 25-26
knowledge, scientific, 26

Lacan, Jacques, 99
language, 61, 86-93
leap of faith, 25
Lennon, John, 36, 40
Locke, John, 17
Logos, 92-93
"love," as word, 88-91

Marburg, University of, 29
mathematics, 15, 16
meaninglessness, 60-63
modern world, crisis of, 1-5, 69, 72-80

nationalism, 102
Nazism, 30, 102
Nietzsche, Friedrich, 21-24, 43
non-Western cultures, 79
Nothing, The, 35-39, 57-58

One, The (The They), 49-59

Parmenides, 7
phenomenology, 27, 42
philosopher-kings, 11
philosophers, ancient Greek, 5-12
philosophy:
  end of, 28, 39
  modern, 13
  self-centered, 48, 68, 71, 73, 79, 94
Plato, 7-12, 33, 39, 41
Pound, Ezra, 30
Pythagoras, 7

racism, 79, 102
radical doubt (Cartesian), 13-16
rationalists, 18
Rickert, Heinrich, 29
Rousseau, Jean-Jacques, 17, 43

Sartre, Jean-Paul, 60, 62-67
scientific approach, 26-28
self, the (Rousseau), 17, 64-65
sensory knowledge, 14-15
slave morality, 23
Socrates, 7
space (Kantian), 19

technology/technological attitude, 1-5, 72-85, 95
thinking (Heideggerian), 28, 39
thinking thing (Cartesian), 16, 41, 48, 65, 68, 70-71, 73-75, 79
thrown-ness, 44-46, 54, 56
time, vs. infinity, 25
time (Kantian), 19

truth:
  absolute, 21-24
  subjectivity of, 25
  universal, 43, 46

Van Gogh, Vincent, A Pair of Shoes, 84-85

Wagner, Richard, 30
will to power, 23-24
Wolin, Richard, 102
words, 87-93
world:
  existence of, 31-33
  framing of, 76-78
  Heideggerian, 46-49
  modern, crisis of, 1-5, 69, 72-80
  technological/utilitarian attitude of humans toward, 1-5, 72-81, 95

Zen, 43